Coming to America

Voices of Teenage Immigrants

John DiConsiglio

SCHOLASTIC INC.
New York Toronto London Auckland Sydney
Mexico City New Delhi Hong Kong Buenos Aires

Cover illustration
Margaret Riegel

Maps
Carol Zuber-Mallison

Copyright © 2002 by Scholastic Inc.
All rights reserved. Published by Scholastic Inc.
Printed in the U.S.A.

ISBN 0-439-12339-9
(meets NASTA specifications)

SCHOLASTIC, READ 180, and associated logos and designs are
trademarks and/or registered trademarks of Scholastic Inc.
LEXILE is a trademark of MetaMetrics, Inc.

1   2   3   4   5   6   7   8   9   10   23   10 09 08 07 06 05 04 03 02

Contents

Introduction

The new student slowly walks into the classroom. Maybe he's looking down. Maybe she's smiling shyly. It is the student's first day in class—maybe his first day in the country. The teen may look a little different from the other students. Perhaps her English isn't quite as good. But once the new student takes his or her desk, you would be hard-pressed to tell which kids in the classroom were born in this country and which ones are new Americans.

This scene happens in almost every classroom in America. Each year, nearly 800,000 immigrants legally enter the United States. As many as 70,000 of them are teenagers. In addition, about 6,000,000 immigrants enter the country illegally, and about 500,000 of them are teenagers. In all, 10 percent of the U.S. population was born in other countries. Most came to the United States for the same reason immigrants have left their homes for centuries: hoping to find a better life for themselves and their families. Some left behind their friends and their loved ones. Many fled poverty and war. Others were trying to escape the prospect of a dead-end future. Some seem to have traded a harsh life in their home country for an even harder life in the United States—one filled with long hours of work for low pay, a confusing new culture, and, too often, **prejudice** and hatred.

But to many immigrants, life in America offers **opportunities** they could never have in other countries. They came to America for economic reasons, for political and religious freedom, for education. Like millions of immigrants from hundreds of countries before them, they came to live the American Dream— the belief that the United States is the land of opportunity, where anyone who works hard can achieve happiness and **prosperity** for his or her family.

"America can be very hard," says Alexis Aguirre, a 15-year-old immigrant from El Salvador. "You are in a new world. You work and work and work. You have to learn a new language and fit in with new kids at new schools. But once you get here, well, you can be anything you want. The possibilities are endless."

All Americans—except Native Americans—have **ancestors** who came from other countries at some point. So that means that most Americans have immigrant roots. Who are today's immigrants? They are your parents, your grandparents, your teachers, your friends. They are your policemen, your doctors, your grocers, your waiters. They are your favorite actors or sports heroes. And they are the kids next to you in class. Or, they are you.

In these pages, you will hear the stories of six teenage immigrants told in their own voices. They come from countries around the globe—from Russia to El Salvador to Iraq. Some are doing great in the United States. Some are struggling. But they have a lot in common. Each left everything behind to start a new life in a strange land.

America has been called a nation of immigrants. This is their story.

The World

A look at where the kids in this book used to live—and where they live now.

NORTH AMERICA

Minneapolis, MN

Detroit, MI

Orange, NJ

San Francisco, CA

Oakland, CA

UNITED STATES

Washington, D.C.

Los Angeles, CA

CENTRAL AMERICA

PACIFIC OCEAN

San Salvador ✪ EL SALVADOR

Cojutepeque

Chiclayo

PERU

Lima ✪

SOUTH AMERICA

ATLANTIC OCEAN

KEY

ALEXIS AGUIRRE
Cojutepeque, El Salvador to Los Angeles, CA

OLGA MALYKH
Ekaterinburg, Russia to Detroit, MI

AHMED HASHEM
Nasria, Iraq to San Francisco, CA

ELAINE ZHANG
Canton, China to Oakland, CA

SALAH MOHAMED
Mogadishu, Somalia to Minneapolis, MN

AZUCENA DE LA ROSA
Chiclayo, Peru to Orange, NJ

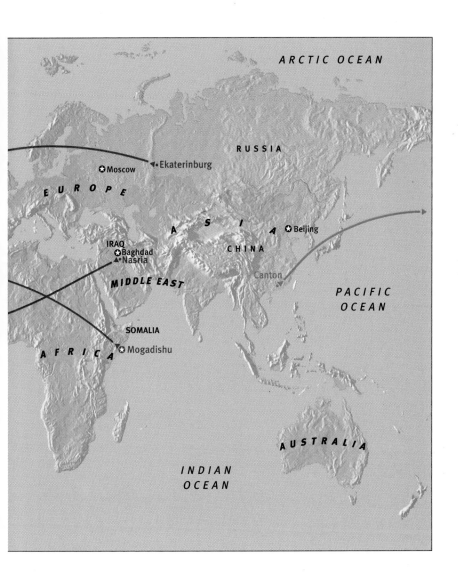

ARCTIC OCEAN

RUSSIA

★ Moscow   ◄•Ekaterinburg

E U R O P E

A   S   I   A   ★ Beijing

CHINA

IRAQ
★ Baghdad
▲•Nasria

MIDDLE EAST

Canton

PACIFIC
OCEAN

SOMALIA

A F R I C A   ✪ Mogadishu

AUSTRALIA

INDIAN
OCEAN

When Alexis was seven years old, he left El Salvador to join his parents in Los Angeles, California. Carrying a charm his grandmother gave him, Alexis traveled for 12 days to reach the U.S.

Mary Gow © Scholastic Inc.

Alexis Otoniel Aguirre
El Salvador

"Where is this place I am going? I thought. I didn't know if I was excited or scared. "

Much of my memory of my homeland is a blur to me. I was very young when I left—just seven years old. But I remember my last day in El Salvador.

I was crying because I was about to leave my grandmother, who was the closest person in the world to me. We were very poor in El Salvador. My parents saved for four years so we could leave. But we could only afford to go one at a time. My father left for the United States two years earlier. For Los Angeles. I barely remembered him. He would write letters and send us money. Then my mother left a year later. And my younger brother left two weeks before I did. I was alone in El Salvador, except for my grandparents. And when my grandmother told me I was going to rejoin my family, I cried.

She tried to make me feel better. She gave me ten dollars to hold on to for an emergency. My grandfather pressed an **amulet** into my hand. In Spanish, we call it *escapulario*. It is a religious medal.

"For you, Alexis," he said, wiping the tears off my cheek. "For good luck and protection in the new world."

I held the *escapulario* tightly in my hand for the 12 days it took me to get to the United States. I had to take two buses through Guatemala, then a truck through Mexico. I wasn't alone. Two of my mothers' friends took care of me. But I was quiet much of the trip. "Where is this place I am going?" I thought. I didn't know if I was excited or scared.

I was born in a little village called El Espinal. The population was maybe a thousand people. Everybody knew everybody else. That's good

Alexis, 16, sits with his brother and parents in their home in Los Angeles. In the U.S., Alexis's parents have to work very hard. "But our family is together," he says, "so we are happy."

Alexis stands in the shadow of Hollywood. After learning English and progressing in school, Alexis says, "Already I have achieved some of what you would call the American Dream."

because families were very close. But it also meant a lot of gossip.

When I was young, my father drank a lot. And neighbors would yell out their windows to my mother, "I saw your husband passed out on the street last night." He was not around for us much. But my mother told me that, when he was, he was good to my little brother and me, that he loved us a lot.

Everyone in El Espinal was poor. Whole families would live in two-bedroom houses— sometimes as many as 30 people. None of the roads were paved. When it rained, the street would be one huge mud puddle.

I would walk three miles everyday to school. It was one room with kids of all ages crammed together. Our school band just had drums made out of cans, and cymbals that were really just two tin pie plates.

Still, every person who owned a house would have a little garden where they would grow their favorite fruits and vegetables. My mother would grow *elote*—corn. Every season, we would have a community garden. There, all the people in the village came together and shared what they grew—tomatoes, peppers, corn. Those gardens are my happiest memory of my homeland.

But I also was a child during our civil war. I don't remember much of it—just warplanes dropping bombs all the time. My mother says she used to put me to sleep under the bed so I wouldn't hear the explosions. She would sit on the ground next to me. Some nights she would tell me about how wonderful our life in the United States would be. I'd lie under the bed, the bombs dropping around us, and she would tell me that in the United States, if you worked hard, you could be anything you wanted.

I don't know how much I understood then. But when I came to the United States, I remember holding my grandfather's amulet and being excited about seeing my mother and my brother.

I didn't know what to think about my father. My mother had told me that he stopped drinking in America. He had a job as a painter and was working hard to make a good home for us.

I didn't remember him at all. I wasn't sure I knew what he looked like. But I recognized him the moment I saw him. I remember running to him and hugging him tight, crying loudly. I didn't let go of him for a very long time.

That night, I took a bath in hot water for the first time in my life. The next day my father took me to buy shoes. During my trip to Los Angeles, I had worn my grandfather's shoes— a man's shoe that was four sizes too big for me.

On my second day here, my mother **enrolled** me in school. I could speak almost no English. But I learned to speak it by sitting in class with Americans every day, just listening to them talk.

Even today, the thing that I love the most about the United States is the **diversity.** I have friends who are Hispanic, Korean, white, black. I have learned that you must try to make everyone your friend—whether they are from your country or speak your language. You can't just say, "I will only be friends with Central Americans." Or, "I will not talk to immigrants." You have to talk to everyone.

And already I have **achieved** some of what you would call the American Dream. My mom gave birth to me when she was sixteen. My dad was twenty-two. She had only a sixth-grade education. And my dad barely finished the ninth grade. But I have already done better than that. I'm in the tenth grade. I want to have a better life than they did. That's why they brought me here. And that's why they work so hard to keep a roof over our heads and make sure we have enough to eat. And if I ever have kids, I want them to have a better life than I. Here, that is really possible.

We are still very poor. I see my father work 15 hours a day to bring us extra money. And I don't like that. But our family is together, so we are happy. I remember that first night here, in that first apartment, all four of us sleeping in the same bed. I couldn't sleep, even after my long, long journey. I was thinking, "What is this strange place my family and I have come to?" My heart was racing. It was like an adventure was about to begin.

El Salvador

El Salvador is the smallest, most densely populated country in Central America. Nearly six million Salvadorans are crowded into an area about the size of Massachusetts. More than half of them work as laborers for low wages.

For decades, the country has been ruled by a small upper class that controlled most of the land. In 1979, tensions between the rich and poor resulted in civil war. Rebels led a twelve-year battle against the U.S.-backed government. More than 75,000 Salvadorans were killed before a 1991 cease-fire tried to unite both sides.

After the cease-fire, El Salvador struggled with poverty and high unemployment. Then in 2001, the country was hit by two devastating earthquakes which killed and injured thousands of people and further damaged the country's economy.

Today, El Salvador is still trying to recover from its painful past and find a way to feed its people.

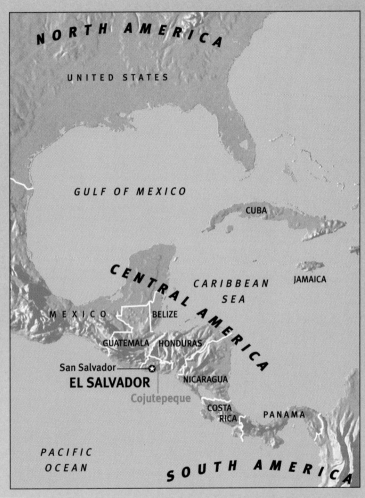

Alexis Aguirre left Cojutepeque, in El Salvador, to move to the United States. El Salvador is located in Central America, and is bordered by Guatemala and Honduras.

Olga moved with her family from Russia to Michigan. "My parents wanted us to have a better life," she explains. Olga is with her parents, Natalya and Sergey, and her brother, Alex.

Olga Malykh
Russia

"When I came here, I had this huge dream of having many American friends. But that has not happened."

I was a waitress this summer. It was the first real job I have had. When I first came to the United States from Russia, I could not work. I wasn't a legal resident yet. I did not have my Green Card. (That's a **visa** that immigrants need to legally live and work in the United States.) But this summer, I had my Green Card, so I worked as a waitress.

It was in a little diner called Coney Island. I know that waitressing is not a job I want forever. But I was just earning some extra money while school was out. And I loved it!

I loved memorizing the menu. I loved all the food you could order—cheeseburgers and French fries and frozen Cokes.

I loved the idea of smiling at people. If you smile at people in Russia, they think there is something wrong with you. But at Coney Island, I would smile at people when I brought them coffee and ask them if they were having a good day. Black people. White people. Russians. Asians. Spanish people. And usually they smile back at you. They can be so friendly.

I was a waitress this summer. And for the first time, I felt at home in America.

My family and I came here three years and three months ago. My father, my mother, my younger brother, and I. And my cat. Her name is Styopia. My brother is 13. His name is Alexander. But at home we call him Sasha. And my parents still call me Olya.

We weren't rich in Russia, but we were doing fine. My father is a computer genius, a software engineer. My mother was a math teacher. But life in Russia is hard now. The economy is very bad. There are no jobs. There are lines for everything. You wait on line for bread. For orange juice. There are no stores like the ones you have here, where you can buy everything. You go to one store for your milk, then you walk two miles and hope another store has fruit. My parents wanted us to have a better life, to go to good schools and have good jobs. Here, my father can make more money. He can even send money back to Russia to help my grandparents.

Before we came to the United States, my mother got a letter from a friend who had moved to a little town in New Jersey. She described it as a place with trees and private houses. I thought all of America would look like that. But we came to Detroit. And Detroit, you know, does not look like that. The city is so big. It has lots of cars. And people move very fast.

But what surprised me the most was how many Russian people there are here. That was very unexpected. I thought there would be only Americans. Sometimes it is like we never left St. Petersburg, a city in Russia. Everyone around us speaks Russian. The other Russian

When Olga was a young girl in Russia, she took art lessons from her mother. Today, art is still an important hobby for Olga.

Olga, 18, Alexander, 14, and their parents, Natalya and Sergey, visit a park in Detroit. In Russia, Natalya was a teacher and Sergey was a software engineer. But jobs were hard to find.

families welcomed us when we first came here. All of my friends are Russian. My boyfriend is Russian, too.

My mother acts like she is still in Russia. She has barely learned English. I must read all her letters to her. She cannot work as a teacher here because her English is poor. So she is a housewife. She likes living with other Russians. It makes her feel at home. But sometimes, I think, she feels that life is flying away.

I know what she means. I, too, feel like something is missing. When I came here, I had this huge dream of having many American friends. But that has not happened. The American boys and girls at school, they are very nice. But it feels fake. They are not really interested in having new friends. When they hear my accent, the conversation kind of dies. And you know you will never get close to them. Their friends are set already and you can't blend in. The Russians, they will accept you. You are one of them.

It is not all the American kids' fault. It is mine too. If I had worked harder, I would have had more American friends. But in some ways, we are so different. American teenagers can be less mature. In Russia, you are a grown-up at 14. Maybe you are working or studying. And soon, you get married.

In the United States you are allowed to stay a kid much longer. Even the way we dress is different. Russian girls wear skirts and heels to school. American kids can go to school in their pajamas. I once heard people say that I was the best-dressed girl in school. I think they were making fun of me. So now I wear blue jeans.

I should have tried to make American friends earlier. But now, I fear something is lost, and I can't go back and get it. I remember when I was in ninth grade, our English teacher gave us an assignment. We had to make a puppet show out of the book *Great Expectations.* She had us work in teams. It was so much fun. I went over to this one girl's house. She wrote the script for the puppet show, and I drew the sets. I remember her mom made us a caesar salad. It was a special experience for me. It was when I still had the hope of making American friends.

But after that, nothing happened. We would see each other in the hallways and say hi. She was with her American friends, and I was with my Russian friends. I still have her phone number. I think about calling her. But she would think it was silly, after all this time, just to call to say hello. Now I have learned my lesson. If I get an American friend I will be happy. But until then, I have the Russians.

I stopped waitressing when the summer was over. My parents want me to focus on my studies. I understand, but I miss it. I know it sounds silly. Who would miss waitressing?

Some nights, I think about what it was like when the booths at Coney Island were filled with people. They are talking so fast and loud. And they are all smiling and happy. All of their voices rise up like one. English and Russian and Chinese and Spanish. It's like music. I take a minute to close my eyes and listen to all these people talking and laughing. I smile and drink it in.

R u s s i a

Russia is a giant nation—in size, history, and importance. It stretches across both Asia and Europe. It is home to more than 100 nationalities and ethnic groups.

In 1919, a revolution turned Russia into the world's first **Communist** country, eventually called the Union of Soviet Socialist Republics. The Communist leaders promised to take power from the rich and give it to the workers. Instead, the government ended up controlling almost everything. Under leader Joseph Stalin, millions who opposed the government were killed.

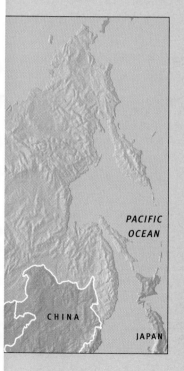

PACIFIC
OCEAN

CHINA

JAPAN

During Stalin's rule, the Soviet Union entered a long period of hostility, known as the Cold War, with the United States. Soviet leaders spent most of the country's money on weapons and the military. The economy suffered. In 1991, the Communist-led government fell apart. The country took its old name back. Since then, Russia has worked toward reforming its government and its struggling economy.

Olga Malykh is from Ekaterinburg, in Russia. Russia stretches across parts of Europe and Asia. It is about twice the size of the United States, with about half as many people.

When Ahmed was a boy, his town in Iraq was bombed by Americans. Later, his family moved to the United States. "For a long time, I wasn't happy in America," he says.

Ahmed Hashem

Iraq

> *"Isn't it strange? The country
> I hated is now my home."*

The Americans dropped bombs on us at night. There was no sleep. Even if we dozed off, five minutes later another bomb would drop nearby. It was crazy. Constant explosions. The sounds of planes flying over our house. Crazy.

We never thought the Americans would attack us. We lived in Iraq. We knew the American president was threatening an airstrike if our president, Saddam Hussein, did not withdraw his troops from Kuwait. This was 1991. I was five, six. I remember my mother and father listening to the news on the radio. We never thought there would really be a war.

And if there was, it would be in the capital, Baghdad. Not in our town. We lived in a small town called Nasria, hours south of Baghdad. We had nothing to do with the invasion of Kuwait. Why would they bomb us?

Nasria was two blocks from a river, and the Americans had targeted the bridges that crossed the river as supply lines. It was insane—nothing ever crossed those bridges but fruit carts. Still, they bombed us throughout the winter.

I remember we had a little heater that ran on oil. My mother put it in the kitchen. It was the only room where we felt safe. There were no windows in the kitchen and no glass to shatter when the bombs fell. All of our family would gather around the stove and hold on to each other. My two little sisters, my aunties, my grandmother and grandfather. All crowded on the kitchen floor. I remember the looks on their faces—how scared they were. And I remember thinking, "I hate America."

Isn't it strange? The country I hated is now my home. It wasn't easy at first. All I knew about America was from cowboy movies. I was

Ahmed, 17, with his sisters Majida, 14, *(left)*; Hanen, 5, *(front)*; and Waad, 12. When the family moved to the U.S., kids teased his sisters for wearing the *hajab*, a traditional head scarf.

expecting big houses on the top of hills and farms. But we moved to San Francisco, where there are a lot of buildings and traffic. For a month or two, I was constantly telling my mother, "I am going back. I don't want to do this. It is terrible here."

My father was a highly respected figure in Iraq. But here, he was sweeping the floor at a liquor store. He was a janitor. It was very hard for him. He had to take care of all of us. He had

Many Americans think Muslims are terrorists, Ahmed says. So he tries to teach kids about his culture and religion. "The more we talk," he says, "the more they change their minds."

to pay for the rent, the food, the bills. And he had to send money back home to his mother and sister and brother in Iraq.

He learned English from renting movies. He would watch them with a notebook on his lap, trying to write down what the actors said. I still have the notebook. Some nights, I flip through the pages and think about what it must have been like for him. He was an intelligent, proud man. And he held a position of respect back home. But in America, he worked as a janitor all day and wrestled with this strange language at night.

When I first came here, the American kids would tease us. I am Muslim and they did not understand my traditions. They would make fun of my sisters for wearing the *hajab,* a head wrap that women wear in my religion. They wear it for respect, to hide their beauty from men. But kids here didn't understand. They would pull at the *hajab.* "Are you bald?" they would tease.

For a long time I wasn't happy in America. I kept thinking that these were the people who had **devastated** my homeland. I remember one night in Iraq, a bomb fell close to our house. My uncle ran to the roof. The building next to us was on fire, just blazing. So he ran out the door. My family screamed at him, "What are you doing? Are you crazy?" He just ran and ran. When he came back, he was crying. He said he had come across a little girl whose family had been killed in a blast. She was badly burned. He ran with her to a hospital. But when he got there, she was dead too.

So many innocent people killed. So many lives ruined. And everyone here seemed to hate me. They think all Muslims are **terrorists.** How was I supposed to live like this?

But you know, somehow, I had the insight to ask myself, "How can I expect people to understand me if I'm not trying to understand them?" I am in a new country now, I told myself. I have to learn about the people here. And they have to learn about me. I decided I would explain myself to other teenagers. If they understood, good. If they didn't, then I would have done the best I could.

Every chance I got, I told kids about my culture, my religion, who I am. The more we talked, the more they started changing their minds. Kids at school were enthusiastic about learning. They wanted to know all about my culture. Everyday they would ask me, "What do your weddings look like? How would you have a birthday party?"

Some of the questions make me laugh. I would have a birthday party the same as anybody else. But I understand that they want to learn. They are opening their minds, too.

I have many American friends now. I have more American friends than Arab friends. As time goes on, Americans understand me more, and I understand them more. I even listen to rap and hip-hop now. I love high school. It's a blast. I love learning about new cultures and **interacting** with new people.

My father thinks I'm a little too American. My friends think I'm a little too Arab. They are all missing the point. I am Iraqi. I am Arab. I am Muslim. And I live in America. I am proud of all that. But most important, I am an individual. There are many people who share all these same characteristics, but even they are different from me. I am myself.

I r a q

Thousands of years ago, Iraq was the site of great civilizations. Today, it is once again a major force in the world. That's because 11 percent of the world's oil lies under its soil. Still, poverty is widespread in Iraq, and the nation cannot produce enough food.

In recent decades, the country has been devastated by two wars. In 1980, an eight-year war with its neighbor Iran bankrupted Iraq.

Then, in 1990, Iraqi President Saddam Hussein invaded neighboring Kuwait, another oil-rich country. A few months later, in January 1991, an international **coalition** led by the U.S. expelled Iraq from Kuwait. The six-week-long clash became known as the Persian Gulf War.

After the war, tensions between Iraq and coalition countries, expecially the U.S. and Great Britain, continued in part because Hussein refused to allow inspectors to search Iraq for weapons.

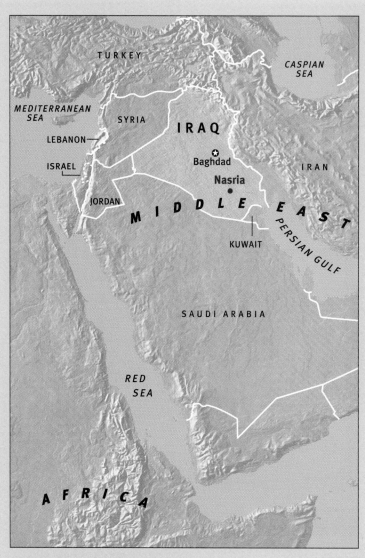

Ahmed Hashem is from Nasria, in Iraq. Iraq is located in the Middle East, and is bordered by Iran, Turkey, Syria, Jordan, Kuwait, and Saudi Arabia.

Elaine Zhang says she's torn between two worlds: China and the United States. "I try to think of myself as American," she explains. "But I cannot forget China."

Mary Gow © Scholastic Inc.

Elaine Zhang
China

"My parents gave up everything to bring me here, and I cannot let them down."

My mother changed when she came to the United States. In China, she was calm and relaxed. In China, she loved me. I would talk to her all the time about boyfriends and school. We would go shopping, and she would always buy me something new. When I was a girl, it would be a toy. As I grew older, she would buy me a scarf or something pretty.

In China, she loved me a lot. She really loved me—not like now.

Here in the United States, we have very little money. At first, my mother and father both worked at a sewing factory. They worked

"My parents wanted me to choose what I could do with my life," Elaine, 20, says. "In China, girls have fewer choices. Most have less than an eighth-grade education."

Elaine *(center)* volunteers at a local organization for low-income women immigrants from Asia.

long hours—sometimes 18 hours a day. And they made four dollars an hour, with no benefits and no breaks. My mother had to change her job because the factory work made her hand go numb. Now, she is a cashier at a supermarket. The factory closed, and now my father has no work.

My mother comes home from the store at night, and she is very unhappy. She sees me. Maybe I am talking on the telephone with my friends. Or maybe I am watching TV or reading the newspaper. So she yells at me. She yells at me because I am not studying. She yells at me because I am not cooking or doing the laundry. She yells at me because I do not have many American friends. She wants me to be 100 percent American. But I will always be Chinese. And she yells at me for that.

When she yells at me, I start crying. I don't know what I did wrong. "Are you my mom?" I ask her. "I don't feel like I am your kid anymore."

She is so unhappy all the time. She is not the same person. I wish we never came here.

Until I was 13, my name was Shu Ling. But we came to Oakland, California, five years ago, and my parents told me I was now Elaine. That was more American, they said. "Only speak English at home," they say. "Only date American boys. You are in America now. Forget China."

But I cannot forget China. I was happy as a child in Canton, a city in the southeast of China. My father owned a restaurant, and he made enough money to take care of us. He thought he could take care of us forever.

We lived in a big house with five rooms, two cars, and a backyard. I didn't think of my studies much. I didn't worry about so many things. I just hung out with my friends. We would go to karaoke or sit around and talk about boys. At home, my father would cook us a meal of mushroom chicken with fish and rice.

I cried for three days when my parents told me we were going to America. I didn't want to leave my friends and my grandmother. My parents tried to explain that under the Communist government my sister and I could never get an education. Most Chinese girls have less than an eighth-grade education. And it can be very difficult for a Chinese girl to go to college. We could never do anything with our lives. My great-great-grandparents had been rich business owners when the Communists took over China. The government stole their home and all their money and made them slave workers on a farm. My parents wanted me to choose what I could do with my life.

I was too young to understand. When we came here, I cried everyday, "Mom, can I go back? Please can I go back?" We live in a tiny apartment with just two rooms. My sister and I share a bed. I had to learn everything over again, like a baby. My ABCs, my 1-2-3s. I was happy when I could finally sing "Twinkle, Twinkle, Little Star." Even the food here was strange—hamburgers, pizza, French fries. In China, we eat rice all the time. Since I have been here, I have gained 30 pounds.

My English was very bad at first, and all the kids at school made fun of me. I remember them saying "Go back to China" and calling me bad names that I didn't understand. But once

I learned English, I saw how friendly Americans can be. In China, there is much competition in school. Other kids will not help you. They want you to do bad so they will look better.

Here, kids help each other all the time. I help some kids with their math, and they help me with my English. I have some American friends now. They want me to take them to karaoke. They say, "You are 18 now. You need to have fun." There are even some American boys who have sent me flowers and want to date me.

But I have no time for fun or boyfriends. I have to focus on my studies. My parents gave up everything to bring me here. I cannot let them down. They want me to be a doctor. I don't even like biology. I want to be a teacher. But when I tell my mother, she yells, "A teacher doesn't make money. A doctor makes money." They think money will make me more accepted here, more American.

I try to see things the way she does. She works so hard, and her boss yells at her. She comes home so tired. There is nothing she can change about that. The only thing she can change is me. If I study harder, I can get a better job and get away from the factories and the two-room apartments and the bad jobs. That, she thinks, will make me more American.

I try to think of myself as American. I can't stay Chinese. None of my friends will like me, and my parents will be so disappointed. So I will try to be American. Many Americans are nice to me now, and I am much happier than when we first came here. But I still feel bad in my heart. Have you ever been hurt? You get better, but sometimes you have scars. I have many scars on my heart.

China

China is the third largest country in the world. And it's home to one billion people—a fifth of the world's population.

Since 1949, China has been under strict Communist rule. Following World War II, leader Mao Zedong began a society that was supposedly ruled by workers and small farmers. Wealthy landowners and the middle class had to give everything to the government. Those who opposed the government were often imprisoned or killed.

Today, the Chinese government has loosened its grip on the economy. Some people have more opportunities than ever. But others still do not. Since 1980, the government has tried to control population growth by making it illegal for families to have more than one child. And political protest is still rarely allowed.

Elaine Zhang is from Canton, in China. Mainland China is approximately the size of the United States. The population of China, however, is about four times that of the U.S.

When Salah Mohamed was 10 years old, heavy fighting broke out where he lived, in Mogadishu, Somalia. "Every day I would hear missiles and gunshots," he says.

Salah Mohamed
Somalia

"*I am Somali, and I am Muslim. But I live in America, and I love it here.*"

When kids come to America from Somalia, they have to make a choice. Are they going to be Somali? Or are they going to be American?

I have seen them. Some kids, they do everything like Americans. They wear clothes like Americans. They date American girls. They stop their prayers and forget their traditions.

Others are not American at all. They don't talk to American teens. They don't listen to American music. If someone asks them to go out to a party, they will say, "My religion doesn't allow me."

I came here from Somalia a year and a half

ago. I still think of myself as Somali—I guess I will always think of myself as Somali. But I watch the Americans, and there is much that I like about them. I like the way they talk and laugh. They have so much freedom and confidence. I like that. I haven't told my mother—she wouldn't approve—but, in many ways, I want to be just like the Americans.

I was born in Mogadishu, the capital of Somalia. It is a different world from here in the United States. The majority of Somalis are Muslim. In Mogadishu, there is a **mosque** on every block—sometimes one on each side of the street. Muslims pray five times a day. I remember hearing the call to prayers: A man would sing from a window at the top of a mosque. I really miss hearing that.

My father was a **merchant** and a religious leader, and we lived happily in Somalia. We weren't rich, but all of our needs were taken care of. We were never hungry, and we had clothes to wear. But the Mogadishu where I grew up doesn't exist anymore. It's all gone now. Because of the war.

Salah, 19, in the traditional Somali robe, called a *kamis*. He wears it on Fridays, the Muslim holy day, and on other important Muslim holidays.

In the early 1990s, **warlords** destroyed our country. I was only 10 when the heavy fighting started. I had no idea what the war was about. But every day I would hear missiles and gunshots.

We lived from day to day, being scared, never knowing if you would be the next one to die. Or if it would be someone from your family. The war hit and, within weeks, everything was gone. There were no more businesses, no more roads, no more cities. It was **desolate**. Everything was wiped out.

As we were planning to leave Somalia in 1992, my father was captured by rebels and held as a hostage for about five days. And then he was killed. We never had the chance to see his body.

In 1993, my family left Somalia for Kenya, a country in east Africa. I went with my mother, my three brothers, and my sister. It was a very hard trip. We took buses and boats and walked a lot. We carried all of our **belongings** on our backs. And there was never enough food. We settled in a **refugee** camp in Bombasa, a city in Kenya. But refugee camps are horrible places. There is little food. Hundreds of people are crowded into tiny tents, and there are many diseases.

The entire time, we wanted to come to the United States. Everyone does. Everyone talks about how good life is here. The schools are good. The people are friendly. You hear that everyone is rich in the United States. There is so much money there, people say, you just have to bend down to pick it up.

My family had applied to come to the United States before we left for Kenya, and it took my mother six years before she got approval. She had a sister in Minneapolis, Minnesota, and a job lined up. She went ahead without us in 1998 and wrote to us every day.

We waited almost two more years before my mother could send for us.

There are two things I remember about coming to America: seeing my mother for the first time in years, and snow. You never see snow in Africa. A lot of rain, but no snow. It is the strangest thing. It's so cold that, just for a

Salah with his mother, Sadia Mohamed, at their home in Rochester, Minnesota. Sadia was in the U.S. two years before she could send for her kids. "She wrote every day," Salah says.

Salah with his family. *Left to right:* Salah's brother, Mohamed, 13; his cousin, Mohamed Isse, 14; his mother, Sadia; his brother, Abdella, 8; Salah; and his sister, Sosia, 11.

moment, you actually think it is hot.

At first, I was very lonely here. And some of the other kids at school were not very nice. They would mock me when they heard me talking in my own language. And they would make fun of how I dressed. For Muslims, Friday is a holy day—like Sundays for Christians or Saturdays for Jews. On Fridays, I would wear a **traditional** robe to school, called a *kamis*. Some kids would tease me. "Why are you wearing a dress?" they would say.

I was depressed at first. But then one of my teachers told me that they just didn't understand my culture. She told me that I shouldn't be angry; I should try to teach them. So when kids asked me why I dressed like this, I would tell them that it's part of my religion. When they asked me why I leave class early, I would tell them that sometimes I go to an empty room and pray.

Suddenly, everyone was very understanding. I must admit, I was surprised. I think when people first meet you, they are shy because they don't understand. But then, after they talk to you, they become much more interested.

I haven't even been here two years and already I have many American friends. American teens are so fascinating to me. So different. American kids in school have fun. They talk back to their teachers. They joke and laugh out loud. In my old school in Somalia, if you talked, they would whip you.

Here, I was very quiet in class at first. I watched the other kids for a while. Then one day I made a joke. I half expected the teacher to take me in the hallway to whip me. But she laughed. And the other kids laughed too. I could barely stop smiling.

The big difference between American teens and Somalis is the dating. I see American kids holding hands and hugging each other. They are kissing each other in public. That doesn't happen with us. We are not allowed to go on dates. We can't hold hands, and we certainly can't kiss in public. To us, that would be disrespectful of our religion.

Still, I am 18. And when you are 18, I don't think it matters if you come from America or

Somalia—or the moon. You think about dating. I have never dated an American girl. It would be strange, and it would upset my mother. I don't want to be disrespectful—not to my mother or my religion or my homeland. But American girls are so filled with life.

I am Somali, and I am Muslim. But I live in America, and I love it here.

Somalia

Somalia stretches for almost 2,000 miles along the northeast coast of Africa. The shoreline is beautiful, but most of the people there live in poverty. About 60 percent of all Somalis make their living herding camels, cattle, sheep, and goats. In 2000, Somalia had the highest rate of malnutrition of any other country in the world.

Somalia has been Muslim for about 900 years. Life for most Somali people centers around places of worship called mosques and religious leaders called imams.

In the 1990s, Somalia was ravaged by war. The north and the south split apart. Wandering armies—led by leaders who called themselves "warlords"—terrorized the nation. Thousands of Somalis fled. The U.S. sent troops. But in 1993, warlords slaughtered 18 American soldiers. The U.S. failed to create order and pulled out after one year. Despite a peace agreement in 2000, much of Somalia is still troubled.

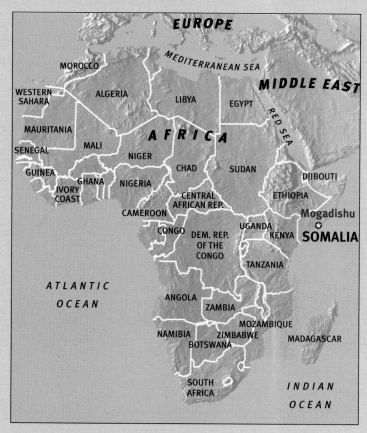

Salah Mohamed is from Mogadishu, the capital of Somalia. Somalia is on the continent of Africa, and is bordered by Djibouti, Kenya, and Ethiopia.

Azucena lived in the U.S. for 15 years before she received a
Green Card. Until then there were many privileges she couldn't
enjoy—like having a job or getting financial aid for college.

Azucena De La Rosa
Peru

"I don't mind being called an illegal alien. It reminds me of the line that I walk. I am neither American nor Peruvian."

The helicopter swooped over our heads, so close that I could feel the wind from its propellers in my hair. We crouched in the tall grass, hoping the pilot wouldn't see us. I was only five, but I remember my mother shouting at my cousin. "Your sunglasses," she yelled. "The sunlight is reflecting off your glasses. They'll find us. Take them off."

We hid facedown in the dirt, motionless for hours. I remember how hot the Mexican sun felt on the back of my neck. I held on to my doll. I was with my mother, my aunt, and my cousin. And the Coyote. That's what you call the man that you pay to help **smuggle** you over the border into California.

My mother had told me that we were leaving our home in Peru to go to Disney World. I was so excited. I packed all my toys. Most of them got left behind in the Mexican hotel room where we met the Coyote and gave him $1,500—just about all the money we had in the world. "Leave everything," he said. All I took with me—in our walk through the deserts and the fields and lying there in the dirt—was that silly little doll.

I must have fallen asleep in the grass. It was dark when my mother **nudged** me awake. I remember I was still half asleep, but I could hear the helicopters, see their flood lights along the field. And I remember hearing the Coyote yell, "Run!"

My mother grabbed one of my arms and the Coyote grabbed the other. They lifted me. It was like I was floating in the air. I remember running and running and running. I kept asking, "How much longer do we have to run?"

In the distance, I could see city lights. My mother said it was San Diego. I thought, We are almost there. But we ran and ran and the lights never got closer. It seemed like it was impossible. We'd never reach those lights.

I am an **illegal alien.** The polite term is "**undocumented** resident." But I don't mind being called an illegal alien. It reminds me of the line that I walk. I am neither American nor Peruvian. I came here from Peru 15 years ago. When people ask me, I say I am Peruvian. But this has been my home for most of my life. I have grown up here. I have gone to school here. I couldn't go back to Peru. I am no longer from there.

Still there are many privileges of America that I don't enjoy. I cannot hold a job. I cannot get aid for college, and we don't have enough money to afford **tuition.** So I ask myself: Am I really American?

We were middle class in Peru. My mother owned a clothing store. We weren't rich, but we weren't struggling for food either. But in my country, you will never move up in life. No

Azucena received her Green Card in May 2001 and was then able to enroll in college. "Sitting in a classroom with other students—that's my American dream," she says.

Azucena would like to study to become a clinical psychologist.

matter how hard you work, there will always be just enough to pay the bills. You will always be waiting for the paycheck to come in.

And then there was my father. He and my mother weren't married, but they had been together since she was fifteen. He promised to marry my mother when she became pregnant with me. Days before their wedding, he called to say that he had fallen in love with another woman, and he was going to marry her instead.

I guess that's why my mother decided to leave. We could have stayed. We had a pretty little house with a nice backyard. There were lots of wildflowers and green grass and trees that gave mangoes and bananas. But my mother had an aunt who had gone to Orange, New Jersey. My mother decided to come here and be with her. My aunt lent her the money to pay the Coyote.

My grandmother made my favorite meal before we left—duck with yellow rice and peas and sweet bananas. I haven't seen her since that night. The next day we took a plane from Lima to Mexico where we met the Coyote. And from there, we made our dash across the border to San Diego, where our aunt met us with plane tickets to New Jersey.

On my very first day in New Jersey, my mother enrolled me in kindergarten. And, from there, we started a normal life. Most people hear "illegal alien" and they think of people hiding in basements and running from the police. But I have never hidden from anyone.

Even if you are illegal, you have to be admitted to public school. So I have been going to school with the same kids from kindergarten through high school. Most of them never knew my **status.** I have American friends and Hispanic friends. I was popular in high school, and my grades were excellent. There is no way to tell the difference between me and someone who was born here.

Well, maybe that's not true. Suddenly, something will come up out of nowhere and slap you in the face. It will make you feel like, even though you grew up here, you really don't belong.

For example, illegal aliens are not allowed

to hold a job. But we still need money. We still have to live. My mother worked as a maintenance person at a day-care center. And I took a job at a clothing shop. I lied to the manager about my name, and I made up a social security number.

I was doing fine until they hired another girl from my school. She turned me in. I couldn't believe she did that. It was so mean. But some people just don't like immigrants. They think we are stealing American jobs.

My stepfather is a citizen. We are trying to become legal residents as his **dependents.** We have been waiting for three years to have our case heard. During my junior and senior years in high school, I kept expecting to get my Green Card. I need it to pay for college. Illegal immigrants can be admitted to college, but they can't get financial aid or scholarships or even a student loan.

I was accepted into a university, and they promised to hold my space until my Green Card came through. But I waited and waited. And finally they had to give the space away.

It's just not fair. It's like they are throwing it in my face—saying, "You are not one of us." I studied hard every night. I loved school more than any other kid in my class. I even enrolled at a community college. I gave them a fake social security number. These courses I am taking, they won't really count. I know I won't be able to get my degree. And they will kick me out of school when they find out. But I love learning. Sitting in a classroom with other students, talking about books or science or psychology. That's my American Dream.

America is called the land of opportunity. And I guess it is, if you fall into certain **categories.** The schools in Peru are not nearly as good as the schools here. Here, I want to be a **clinical psychologist.** If I said that in my old country, they would laugh at me and tell me to find a husband.

But there is a trade-off. My family is not as close here as we were in Peru. In Peru, we all ate breakfast together every morning— mothers, aunts, uncles, grandparents. Here, we are all too busy to sit down to breakfast. Here, everything seems to revolve around working and making money. So you trade being close to your family for living better and having more clothes and being able to give your kids more than one pair of sneakers.

Is it worth it? Sometimes I think maybe it isn't. But then I imagine how it will feel when the gates really open for me, when I can go to school and be whatever I want to be. When I can really be an American. Is it worth it? Deep down in my heart, I know it is.

Azucena received her Green Card several months after she gave this interview.

Peru

Peru's soaring mountains and dense jungles hide a rich history. The Incas ruled an empire there during the 11th century. Great stone ruins from their civilization still cling to the sides of the Andes Mountains. And their descendants still live in the rugged region.

In the 1500s, the Spanish conquered the Incas and mined Peru for gold. Today, their descendants still live in Peru's coastal cities.

During the 1980s, Peru was **dominated** by a small number of wealthy landowners. Terrible unemployment kept the rest of the country in poverty. Since then, life has improved for poor Peruvians. But education and employment levels remain low. And the government still struggles to control corruption.

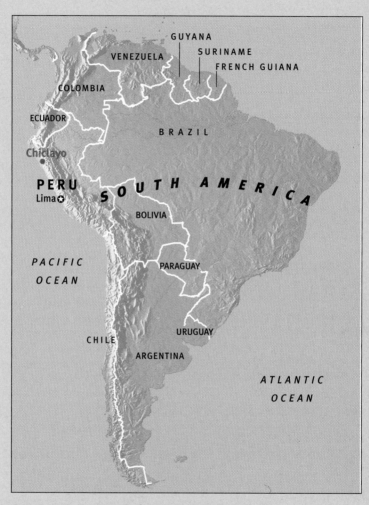

Azucena De La Rosa is from Chiclayo, in Peru. Peru is on the continent of South America, and is bordered by Ecuador, Colombia, Brazil, Bolivia, and Chile.

Glossary

achieve *(verb)* to do something successfully

amulet *(noun)* a charm

ancestor *(noun)* a member of your family who lived before you

belonging *(noun)* something that you own

category *(noun)* a group of people or things that have something in common

clinical psychologist *(noun)* someone who works in the mental health field

coalition *(noun)* a group with a common purpose

communism *(noun)* a way of organizing a country so that all the land, houses, factories, etc., belong to the government or community, and all the profits are shared by all

dependent *(noun)* a person who is looked after and supported by somebody else

desolate *(adjective)* deserted

devastated *(adjective)* very badly damaged or destroyed

dominate *(verb)* to control or rule

diversity *(noun)* a variety

enroll *(verb)* to join or sign up for

illegal alien *(noun)* someone who is living in a country without official permission

interact *(verb)* to spend time with and communicate with others

merchant *(noun)* someone who sells goods for profit

mosque *(noun)* a building used by Muslims for worship

nudge *(verb)* to give someone or something a small push

opportunity *(noun)* a chance to do something

prejudice *(noun)* an unreasonable or unfair opinion about someone based on the person's race, religion, or other characteristic

prosperity *(noun)* success

refugee *(noun)* a person who is forced to leave his or her home because of war, persecution, or a natural disaster

smuggle *(verb)* to bring people or things into a country illegally

status *(noun)* a person's rank or position in a group or society

terrorist *(noun)* someone who uses violence and threats to scare people into obeying

traditional *(adjective)* describing a belief or practice that has been done in the past

tuition *(noun)* payment to attend a college or other kind of school

undocumented *(adjective)* lacking official papers or permission

visa *(noun)* a document giving permission for someone to enter or work in a foreign country

warlord *(noun)* a leader who rules by force